CW00572011

THE MINERS AND COAL LEVELS OF GWENT

COLIN SPENCER

The History Press

In memory of Adam Everley, 1970-2009

First published 2009

The History Press
The Mill, Brimscombe Port
Stroud, Gloucestershire, GL5 2QG
www.thehistorypress.co.uk

ISBN 978 0 7524 5251 7

Typesetting and origination by The History Press
Printed in Great Britain

CONTENTS

ACKNOWLEDGEMENTS

I would like to thank everyone who helped me accumulate all the information that went into the publication of this book: John Henry Smith, Adam Everley, Tony Cooke, Kai Michael and the staff of Gwent Records, Merthyr Tydfil Library, Tredegar Library, David Warren and Gerry Plant (both ex-mine owners), Dave Clarke MBE (Coal Authority), Wayne Hopkins and the Ordnance Survey. I would also like to thank The History Press for publishing this book.

INTRODUCTION

What is a level? A level is a drift or heading driven into the side of a hill or mountain. A lot has been published about the deep mines of Gwent but very little about the levels. I was a deep miner myself but I knew very little about the levels, so in the years before they closed I set out to photograph a few, and I have concentrated solely on the levels in Gwent. A level could be anything from a one-man operation to occupying 100 or more. The coal could be brought out of the mine in a variety of ways; a dram could be pushed by a miner or pulled by a horse or a stationary engine on the surface could be used to pull a journey of drams. In later years a conveyor belt was often used.

I also wanted to find out abut the old levels that were closed long ago. When I finished work I bought myself a digital camera and went looking around Gwent; I found some beautiful remains and I hope you will enjoy the photographs. I refer to the workings as 'levels' although some were called collieries or mines; they were all the same in that they had openings driven into the hill or mountain rather than sinking a shaft as in the deep mines. A tram, or 'dram' as it's known locally, is a container which runs on rails and is used for the transportation of coal and supplies into and out of the levels.

This book is a brief photographic history of the levels, interlaced with information, maps and plans. I apologise if I am not 100 per cent accurate.

The first chapter deals with the levels that were operational in the 1980s and includes photographs of both surface and underground workings. The names of the miners and the owners of the horses are given where known. There are also underground plans of certain levels.

The second chapter covers the much older levels, and gives their locations, owners, numbers employed, deaths and wages. Also included in this chapter are extracts from the Royal Commission for the Employment of Children, 1842, which makes very interesting reading.

The final chapter looks at the last remaining working levels in Gwent, and reminds us that they may be the last generation to extract coal using the techniques and methods of their forefathers.

OLD LEVELS ARE DANGEROUS AND NO ATTEMPT SHOULD BE MADE TO ENTER THEM.

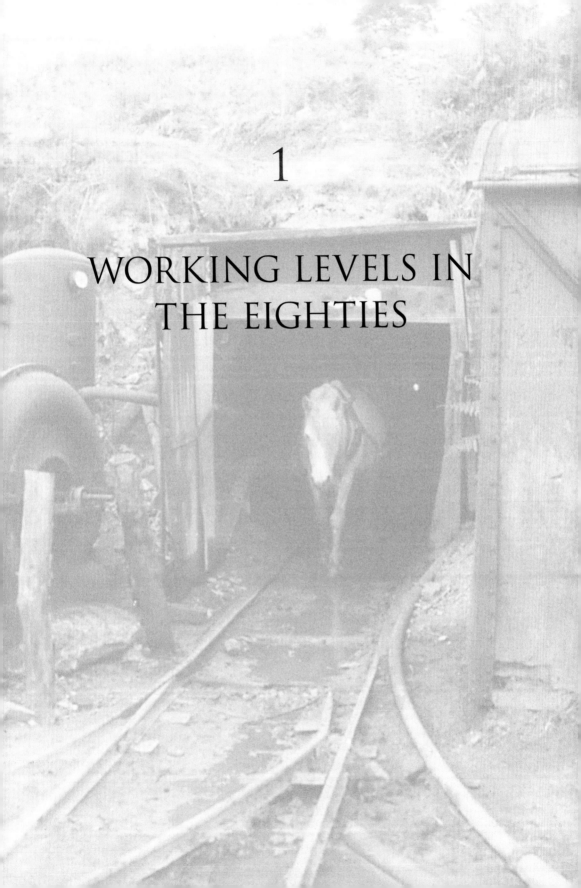

1
WORKING LEVELS IN
THE EIGHTIES

Although the coal industry was in decline in the eighties, with the big strike over and the deep mines folding like a pack of cards, there were still a number of small mines or levels around Gwent. We start the book around the Newbridge Treowen area where the Bush Level was located. The level had a number of owners over the years. A map of 1879 shows the first Bush Level as disused, with an incline from the level down to a tramway. This tramway ran from the Kendon Level past the Bush then beyond Twyn-Gwyn and Cwmdows Colliery, eventually joining Benjamin Halls Tramway. In 1811 the tramway from the Kendon Level had been approved by John Llewellin, on the estimate of P. David to form and stone the proposed line from Newbridge to Kendon at 3s per yard. The Bush was in existence in 1867 when it was advertised for auction with a lease dated 19 November 1865, but it may have existed previously. The first appearance in the lists was in 1873, but in 1908 it disappeared, returning to the list between 1919-1920, and finally from 1923 until 1990. Some of the owners of the level were J. Edwards, Pantysgawen Farm and the Bush Company. In 1923 Lyn Glo Colliery Co. Ltd owned the level with a workforce of seventeen miners underground and five on the surface. In 1934 the Bush Level had twenty men underground and five on the surface. The manager was T.G. Holder under the ownership of the Newbridge Colliery Co., producing 10,000 tons of coal. In 1974 Gerry Plant purchased the mine and worked it up until 1990. The level finished working and the headings were filled in the following year, still under the ownership of Gerry Plant, who by this time had purchased the Penyrheol Level.

Bush Level. This is the surface of the last of the Bush Levels with all the equipment needed to run a mine. In the foreground is one of two entrances with the rails heading down into the mine. In the distance can be seen the tops of the houses of old Treowen. This is where the first of the levels started; the machine on caterpillar tracks housed the winch that pulled the drams out of the mine.

Above and opposite below: The two entrances into the level. One would be the intake where the air went into the mine, around the workings and back out the other opening, called the return road. The dram in one entrance is just disappearing down into the level.

This map, from around 1879, shows the area around Newbridge in the Ebbw Valley. The village remains today, but is much larger. On the map you can see the tramway mentioned earlier which ran from the Kendon Mine past the Bush Level and Cwm Dows Colliery, eventually joining Halls Road Tramway.

We are now looking at a piece of history. This was an air pit to the workings; you will not see this in any modern levels but in the older levels there were quite a few dotted around Gwent. It served two purposes: first it allowed the circulation of the air around the workings and secondly it could be used as an emergency way out.

This air pit had a metal ladder to enable the men to climb out of the level. You can see the rock they went through to sink this pit, and this particular air pit was 92ft deep.

We are now going into the mine; this entrance had a mixture of metal arches and wooden posts.

The second entrance had quite a steep incline and used wooden posts. The dram had just been lowered to the bottom of the incline.

You are now looking at what we in the deep mines called the 'face rippings', the waste or stone above the coal. Some of this waste would be used to fill the space where the coal had been extracted as it was of no use to the owner. Also in this photograph you can see quite a few hydraulic props. These types of props could be used over and over again as opposed to the wooden props which you may only be able to use once. In the deep mine where I worked, we had two different types of these props; one was called the Dobson, the other the Doughty prop. Note also the weight that has come on a section of the timber, causing it to split.

Opposite above: The miner is at the coal face and is using a pneumatic pick to get at the coal. Also in the photo, the hydraulic prop has a curved pipe hanging from it, used to raise and lower the prop.

Opposite below: Only wooden props are in use on this part of the face. The seam of coal at the Bush was top coal 3ft in thickness and bottom coal just under 2ft in thickness.

Gerald Plant, the owner's son, filling a dram. The coal seam here was not very thick but a certain height in the roadway had to be maintained for a number of reasons. Firstly there had to be room for the drams and horses to travel, and in later years it was dictated by regulations.

The miner in this photograph has barely enough room to kneel properly.

When this photograph was taken this miner was using the hatchet with great care, being in such a confined space. The blast bag, the small flexible pipe in the foreground which carried the compressed air which operated the pneumatic pick, had a hole in it and the miner was cutting the damaged part off. When you worked in a level you had to turn your hand to anything.

This is a place in the mine that very few people have seen; it is a pit underground from the bottom seam of coal to the top seam. Although this pit shows a ladder to climb up, Gerry Plant, the last owner, said in the old days there would only be hand and foot holds to climb up. There were a number of these pits underground in the Bush Level, the distance between the two seams being six to seven yards. The old miners would climb up these pits, work a section of coal then drive another one further on. This way they could obtain some of the top and bottom seam of coal from one level.

Opposite: On the opposite page is a plan of part of the workings of the Bush Level, and on it you can see the pits I have mentioned. At the bottom of the plan, labelled 'Old Level', is where the first Bush started. The workings of the Bush started near the old railway line by old Treowen and finished just short of the lane that goes from Croespenmaen to Treowen.

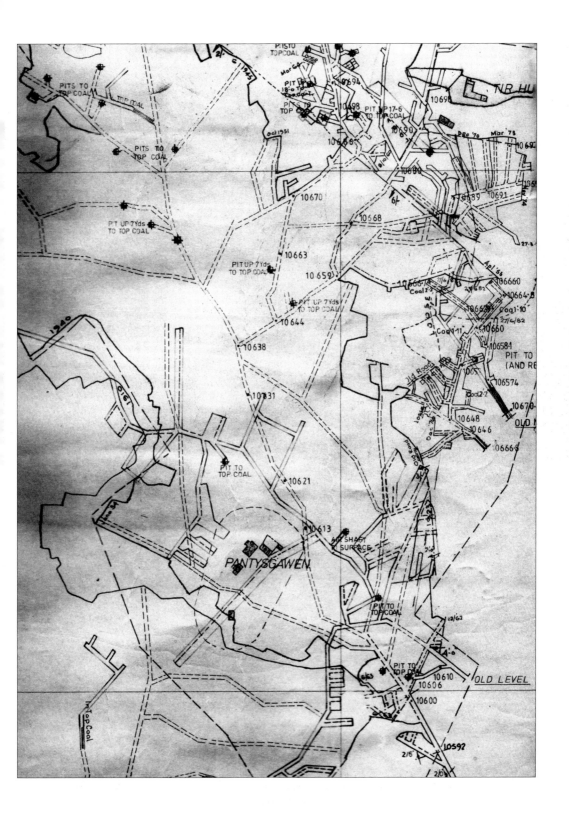

Left: We are now in the old workings of the Bush Level, and it differs from the previous photographs as there are no supports holding the roof; you can get away with this if there is solid ground as the old miners who worked in the house coal mines can remember. The rails have been left in place.

Below: This is part of the old workings of the first Bush, so we could be as far back as the nineteenth century. Again, there are no supports.

Pentwyn Level, situated on the west side of the valley overlooking Llanhilleth in the Ebbw Valley. At the time this level was owned by Tom Wilcox. To the left of the photograph you can see a track which led to the village of Trinant. The level closed in 1992.

In this photograph we can see the surface of the mine with the screening system, along with two empty drams. The entrance to the level is just visible in the centre of the photo.

Above left: The other entrance or exit out of the mine.

Above right: The men have started to form a new entrance. Although modern machinery dug this cutting, the timber work is the same as practiced many years ago.

Opposite: Horses were used a lot in the mines of South Wales and in this photograph the horse with a dram full of coal is emerging from the level. On the left of the entrance is part of the apparatus to pump the compressed air into the mine.

The horse underground is patiently waiting with its harness on, ready to be attached to the dram.

Opposite: For those who have never been underground, this is a junction where one heading goes straight on while the other goes to the right, or if need be to the left. If you wanted the dram to go straight on you would close the latch on the right-hand side and open the other one. If you wanted the dram to go to the right you would close the latch on the left and open the right-hand one. The latch, or points, is the short pointed rails in the photo just before it bends around the corner, the same principal as the modern railway except on a smaller scale and done by hand.

Two miners having a chat. One is the collier Adrian Summers, the other is the haulier Branwell Clive Dee.

The time for talking is over, and Adrian is filling the dram with the coal which Branwell will take to the surface. To the right of this photograph, but out of sight, is Les Corrigan working on the coal face.

I think this photograph of Les Corrigan shows what a lot of people think a typical miner used to look like. In a lot of mines you came to work in your clothes, worked your shift then went home in the same clothes. It would be very rare to have showers at the level, as it was in the deep mines until they installed the pit head baths.

Les is here at the coal face filling a small tub ready to be pulled down the face to the main heading where Adrian Summers (shown in the previous photos) would load it into the dram.

The Big Arch Level. We now switch valleys and are in the Afon Lwyd Valley by the British Tal-y-waun between Pontypool and Blaenafon. You are looking at the entrance to the mine and in the background you can see the spoils of the old mine workings of many years ago which included deep mines, levels and balance pits. The rope in the centre of the rails seems to be out so the drams must be inside the mine. This mine had showers for the miners, which was very unusual.

Opposite above: You can see the amount of timber this particular mine used. In the distance by the trees (although not visible) is the second entrance to the mine. Up on the top of the banking to the left of the photograph is where the main railway line from Pontypool to Brynmawr used to run.

Opposite below: As you look at the photographs in this book you will see the slightly different shapes of the drams used and this photograph shows a fine example of the type of dram used at this mine.

This is the second entrance to the mine, which I mentioned earlier. The men are pushing the dram to the entrance, where it will be attached to a rope then lowered into the mine using a stationary engine that is on the surface.

The end of the day – time to pack up and go home.

Viv Griffin was the owner of the mine at the time and here he is with the surveyor and workmen looking at the plans of the mine.

I can't say a lot about this photograph other than when I took it the collier was having a breather.

In this photo we can see the miner using a sledge to knock in what we in the deep mines called a dog nail – a metal pin driven into the wooden sleeper which the rails rest on and stops them from moving around.

Mine official and miner looking at the small pump used to extract the water out of the mine. Water could always be a problem in the deep mines and the levels. Some of the levels photographed did not have this problem but those that did solved it in different ways. If the coal seam went to the rise the water drained away naturally, otherwise pumps would have to be installed.

We are still looking at the official and miner but we are over the top of the rise and you can see the water coming out of the pump and flowing away to the old workings. Up on the left of the photo you can see a flexible pipe called an air bag which carried fresh air into the workings.

Penyrheol Level. This level was on the mountainside behind Cefn-crib Chapel and the Star Inn on the mountain road which ran from Hafodyrynys to Pantygaseg and Pontnewynydd. It was purchased in 1984 by Gerry Plant. It closed in 1995.

Opposite: A mine official testing for gas. I'm not sure how much gas was detected in the levels but safety always came first, as it was in the deep mines. I think the owner could nominate himself to perform these duties, but later on there had to be a person with a certificate to use a flame safety lamp.

Two more photographs which show the surface of the mine. The drams in the lower photo are empty, ready to go back into the mine.

This is the same level, only they have driven two new openings.

When you look at this photo, just inside of the opening you can see a bar reaching from the top of the arches to the bottom. This was a safety apparatus in case the drams ran away from the surface and down the incline into the mine.

I have previously mentioned the safety bar, and in this photo you can see it clearly. The bar was raised to allow the drams to pass then dropped back down as a safety precaution, just in case a dram on the surface ran away and there were men working just inside of the mine. We in the deep mine I worked at called this bar a 'Warick'; other mines may have had a different name. In the new heading you can already see the water they will have to worry about.

The haulier, having just come out of the mine with a dram of coal, is pushing on the dram around the turn in case it jumped the rails.

Another haulier with a different horse coming out of a different entrance to the mine.

Opposite: Horses played a big part in the coal industry. This horse, whose name was Sam, is waiting just inside of the mine ready to take the empty dram back to the colliers at the coal face.

The black horse, whose name was Darkie, is waiting while the collier fills the dram. Also in the photo you can see the protective head gear on the horse.

This photograph could be classed as a typical mining scene of years ago. The horse's harness is being attached to the dram by the haulier, the collier has just filled the dram, and his number chalked on the dram. Note the rails, the wooden supports with the sides packed, and the protective head gear on the horse.

Opposite above and below: In the old days of mining the colliers had their own number to identify them. When they filled the dram they wrote this number on the side. This number helped the management keep track of how much coal each miner had filled, and they were paid accordingly. In the old days in the deep mine they did not get paid for small coal.

Left and below: A lot of level work was done on your knees, as you can see in these two photographs. This led to a lot of miners developing health problems in later life.

Collier Mike Desmond filling a dram which has seen better days.

Mike's father, Bill Desmond, going to get some tools.

Above: When you worked in a level, you had to turn your hand to most jobs. Bill Desmond is preparing to lay down a junction in the heading; some of the rails will go straight on while other rails will go around the turn. In his hand is the measuring bar and in front of him is what we called in the deep mines 'the cross'. By his right foot is the 'Jim Crow', which was used to bend or straighten the rails. I have included a small photo to show what a 'Jim Crow' looked like (*right*). A bar would be inserted, then the spindle would turn, come out and push against the part of the rail you wanted to bend or straighten.

Rithan Mine, deep inside the old opencast workings above Llanhilleth. There were actually two levels in the remains of the opencast. Rithan Mine was owned by David Warren who named the mine after his two children, Richard and Nathan. David opened the mine on the 5 November 1980; previously he owned and worked the Swffryd Level which he bought from Tommy Goff in 1974. When he finished with the Swffryd, he opened the Rithan and worked it until 1990. He then sold it on and the mine carried on working for a few more years.

Opposite above: The dram of coal has just come out of the mine where a rope will be attached to pull it up a small incline to be tipped.

Opposite below: The dram has been pulled up the incline by a small winch and tipped. At first the winch was driven by compressed air but later on David Warren, the mine owner, purchased a winch driven by diesel.

In some of the mines the drams had an opening at the back or front which you unbolted to enable the coal to be removed when it was tipped, as you can see in this photo. The coal was then allowed to slide down the shute which had different size holes in it for grading.

Opposite: When you look at this photograph you see the size of the timber used at this level. It varied from level to level, but generally the small timber was used to pack the sides and top of the roadway props.

This scene in this photograph could be a century years old, a fine example of a pair of timbers at the entrance to the level. In the deep mines we called this a collar and arm; the uprights were the arm and the timber across the top the collar. When speaking to the owner, David Warren, he said the only thing that changed in 100 years of working in a level was the introduction of compressed air and electric lights. Note the amount of rock above this entrance.

We are now at the entrance to the level; the metal arches are well strutted, with the sign above telling you that this is a safety mine, so no smoking or naked lights.

David Warren, the owner, is the miner in this photograph holding the horse.

A photograph that shows Bernard O'Reilly and Stan Stadden working as a team. To work as a team and to get on with one another was important, as each miner's safety was effectively in the other's hands. Plus, you may spend more time with your buttie than with your wife!

Haulier Paul Lyons and his horse, Charlie. At least in the levels the horse saw daylight every day, unlike the horses in the deep mines.

I mentioned previously about a pair of timbers; you can see a fine example of the notched timber around the collier, who has his wet gear trousers on. In the old days it would have been all timber work throughout the level but, as some of the previous photographs show, modern metal arches were used – especially near the entrance to the level. This type of timber-work was called 'Welsh knotched', set at an angle to allow for the weight that would come on them. The timber at this level came from the forestry by Aberbeeg Hospital.

Two colliers, Bernard and Stan, going about their work. In the lower photo one is using a square mouth shovel which was ideal on smooth bottoms, the bottoms being the floor of the level.

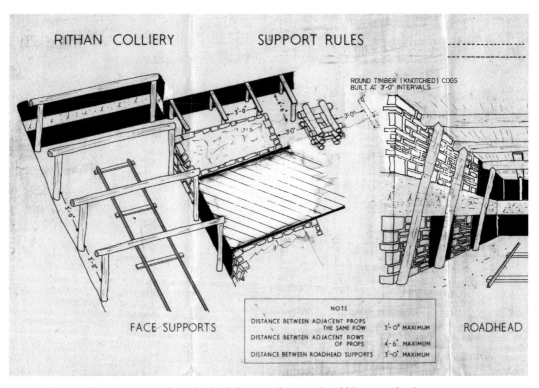

ROUND TIMBER (KNOTCHED) COGS
BUILT AT 3'-0" INTERVALS

FACE SUPPORTS

NOTE		
DISTANCE BETWEEN ADJACENT PROPS THE SAME ROW	3'-0" MAXIMUM	
DISTANCE BETWEEN ADJACENT ROWS OF PROPS	4'-6" MAXIMUM	
DISTANCE BETWEEN ROADHEAD SUPPORTS	3'-0" MAXIMUM	

ROADHEAD

Rithan Colliery support rules, which I believe each mine should have on display.

Opposite: Waiting patiently for the haulier to come back is Charlie. The horses were generally well looked after. In the early days, the owner of the mine thought the horse was more valuable than the men.

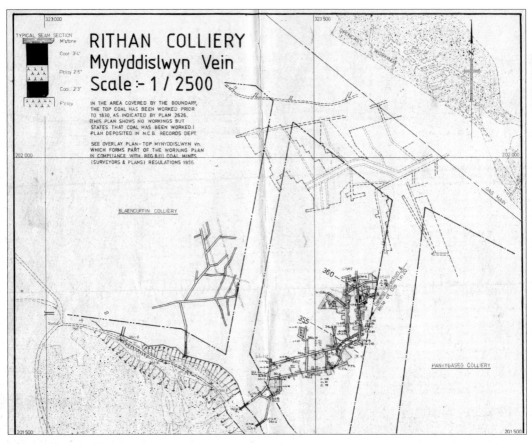

RITHAN COLLIERY
Mynyddislwyn Vein
Scale :- 1 / 2500

TYPICAL SEAM SECTION

IN THE AREA COVERED BY THE BOUNDARY,
THE TOP COAL HAS BEEN WORKED PRIOR
TO 1830, AS INDICATED BY PLAN 2626.
(THIS PLAN SHOWS NO WORKINGS BUT
STATES THAT COAL HAS BEEN WORKED.)
PLAN DEPOSITED IN N.C.B. RECORDS DEPT.

SEE OVERLAY PLAN- TOP MYNYDDISLWYN Vn.
WHICH FORMS PART OF THE WORKING PLAN
IN COMPLIANCE WITH REG 8(1) COAL MINES
(SURVEYORS & PLANS) REGULATIONS 1956.

BLAENCUFFIN COLLIERY

PANTYGASEG COLLIERY

I finish the Rithan Colliery with a plan showing the workings in January 1981, and the position where the Pantygaseg and Blaencuffin Collieries were situated. Also on the plan is part of the Blaencuffin workings and the entrances.

Pantygaseg Colliery again, deep inside of the old opencast workings. The owner at this time was John Desmond, with a workforce of about four or five men. In the background is where the entrance to the mine was, and in the foreground a new heading was being driven towards the boundary of the Rithan Colliery.

This is the new heading I mentioned in the previous photo.

I think that by looking at this photo you can see the amount of waste that was extracted to get at the coal seams.

The haulier and his horse have just emerged from the mine with a dram full of coal. The haulier walking in front of the horse has no need to look back because he knows the horse will follow him.

The dram has been emptied and the haulier is once again in front of the horse, walking back into the mine to deliver the empty dram to the colliers at the coal face.

Opposite above: A photograph showing the haulier Billy Smith and his horse, Danny, inside the mine.

Opposite below: A miner sawing small timber that he will use to pack the sides and top of the roadway.

Above: It's time for a break, a cup of tea from a flask perhaps. Notice the way they are resting, not sitting but crouching down with the weight more on the one leg than the other; the old miners will remember this.

Left: Break over and back to work. Some of the waste is being used to pack the side of the roadway. The more you got rid of, the less you had to transport out of the level and dump.

I end the Pantygaseg Level with a photograph which shows everything that the old levels or deep mines were about; you have the horse with its harness and protective head gear shackled to the dram, the collier filling an old fashion looking dram, a shovel standing on the side of the roadway, the timber supports knotched, and the rails in the foreground. I think a lot of the older miners can associate themselves with this picture. The hours may have been longer, the wages certainly not as much and the work just as dirty and dangerous, but you could not beat the comradeship.

We are now at the other end of the opencast from the previous level, going towards St Illtyd Church above Llanhilleth; this is Blaencuffin Level. There was a level of this name as far back as 1801, and in 1832 Thomas Powell and Thomas Protheroe worked the Blaencuffin vein. Two years later Protheroe carried on alone, leasing the coal under Llanhilleth Farm for a period of twenty-one years. This particular level was near the top of the mountain and was owned by Sid and Dennis Williams, two brothers. In this photograph a journey of drams full of coal is emerging out of the level, pulled out by a stationary engine driven by compressed air.

The empty drams are on their way back into the mine. The rest of the photograph is typical of the surface of the small mines.

A lone miner walking away from the entrance to the mine.

Karee Thomas Williams, Kenneth Sid Williams and surface worker Dennis Hatchet are going about their business.

The dram of coal has been tipped down the screening tray ready to be loaded into bags or a lorry, ready for distribution.

It's the end of the day, the mine gates are closed and locked and the miners have gone home after another hard day's work.

This was the second way out of the mine when I took this photograph, but the Mines Inspector was not satisfied, so later on they drove another heading a little further on down the track which you can see in the foreground. If you followed this track on down you would come to the Rithan Mine in the opencast; on the plan of the Rithan you can see the entrances.

Dennis Williams is ripping the coal down with the pneumatic pick while Kenneth Williams, his nephew, is ready with the shovel to load it into the dram. As you can see this was a good thickness of coal compared to some of the other levels.

Opposite above: We are now inside the mine. Dennis Williams, the co-owner, is starting to make a pair of timbers. When you used the hatchet you made sure that it was kept sharp. One of the jobs I did in the deep mine was to sharpen the hatchet every day.

Opposite below: Karee Williams and Tom Morgan are checking the rails, the timber supports beginning to bend with the weight on them.

Sid Williams using the mandril, with a pick or puncher in the foreground; you can see the marks left by the pick. As you can see the coal was worked up on the ledge, then you came behind and cut the bottoms, the waste below the coal, to make the necessary height.

The old second way out which I mentioned earlier. This was the inside of it, with two abandoned axles and wheels and a fair drop of water.

This photograph shows the amount of water in this particular mine; the water is dripping from the roof and coming up from the floor. Luckily, although the entrance to the mine was in a dip, the coal went to the rise so in the dip they drove a small adit. The water flowed out of the mine, went out the adit and down the side of the hill. This saved the expense of installing a pump. Also note the timbers beginning to bend. The Blaencuffin Mine eventually closed in 2001, 200 years since the first mine with that name opened.

2

ANCIENT LEVELS

In this chapter I have concentrated on the levels that were in existence as far back as the nineteenth century. There were hundreds of small mines or levels around Wales, with quite a few in Gwent. I was born in a village called Treowen, near Newbridge, in what was then Monmouthshire, and within half a mile either side of the village there were levels such as Cwmdows, Ty-brachty, Ty-mawr, Twyn-gwyn No. 1 and No. 2, Bush, Rhiw, Orchards, Kendon, Millbrook and Rosemount. If you extended it to a mile you could double the number. The hills and the valleys in the coal belt are honeycombed with tunnels from these levels and deep mines.

In 1842, a paper was published titled 'The Royal Commission Reports into the Employment and Conditions of Children in Mines and Manufactories'. This is a small extract:

Gwrhay and Pen-y-van, collieries, parish of Mynyddislwyn,

Adults	59
Under 18 years of age	14
Under 13 years of age	13

Aaron Crossfield Esq., part proprietor.

Our mines are worked by levels, we employ no machinery whatever, the coals are brought out from the workings by horses along tram-roads, our main road is six and a half feet high, and the mine is well ventilated by air-ways and air pits.

Moses Williams age 7, air door boy.
Father carried me down 18 months since, he brings me in the mornings and I return with him at night.

Rosser Jenkins age 8, collier.
Works with father as often as he works, sometimes takes bread and cheese with him and drinks the water below.

John Evans age 8, collier.
Father took me down to claim a dram, has often fallen asleep, father pulls me up when he wants me.

Mrs Mary Lewis
My husband has worked in these mines many years I have 12 children six of whom are working in the mines.

Court-y-bella and Manmoel Collieries, parish of Mynyddislwyn, Sir Thomas Phillips and co; Occupiers.

Males Employed.	
Adults	90
Under 18 years of age	30
Under 13 years of age	10

Coal brought through level by horses and conveyed by incline plane to the Tram road, the ascending carts worked by balance wheel.

Mr Hananiel Morgan agent to Sir Thomas Phillips and co.

Males only are employed in this part of the country in the mines and many young boys are taken as soon as they can stand on their legs.

Henry George 7 years old, collier.

Twelve months below assists Davy Jones to pick as father works in level, takes bread and cheese down.

Thomas Jenkins 10 years old, collier.

Father took me down to claim his dram when I was six years old, I work with John Jones who pays my father 2s 6d a week for my labour.

Joseph Roberts 13 years old, collier.

Was six years old when first taken into the mine, goes to work at three and four in the morning and returns at four five and six at night.

George Roberts 11 years old, collier.

Been five years in the coal mine and works with brother, bores the holes in coal for blasting.

Mr Samuel Jones cashier and clerk to Waterloo Colliery Level, when work is dull the fathers carry the boys below ground when four or five years old.

Wages varied in the levels

David Jones age 17 haulier earns 13s a week,

David Williams age 10, collier earns 2s 6d a week.

James Harper age 20, collier earns 18s to 20s a week.

Edward Lewis blacksmith to the Traenent colliery, my wages are 21s a week.

When I worked in the deep mines you were paid in cash at the pit or it went into the bank. The year this report was written you might have your wages in cash or you could be paid by the truck-system or company shops – you did not have cash in your hand, what you earned was credited in the shop. When you wanted something like food or clothing you went to the shop, then it was taken off your credit. As the mine owners owned the shop they could charge you what they liked. Paying the workmen in this way enabled them to cut down the cost of working their coal, as they were able to make a profit on the foodstuffs and other necessities of life which the workers were obliged to buy from them.

A report in 1829 into the paying of workmen's wages in goods stated that the practice was common in the hills of Monmouthshire. However, the payment was sometimes made in ale so that the other tradesmen like shoemakers etc. were unable to obtain payment.

This is just a small extract showing what life was like in the nineteenth century but I think you can tell it was a very hard life. Going underground into the deep mines when I started work at sixteen or seventeen was scary enough, but to start when you were five or six years old, one can only imagine how these children felt. They would be underground for hours and hours, with perhaps only a candle for light by which to work. The next time the electric power fails at your home and you light a candle while waiting for the power to come back on, give a thought for these children that worked in that dim light. Looking back at my old records, a lot of the old miners in the deep mine had to finish work with a complaint called nystagmus, which was caused by working in bad light. It was not only boys or men employed, girls and women also worked in the mines. In 1842 the Mines Act came into power, and from the first day of March 1843 no females be employed, nor males under ten years of age.

The names of the levels were something again, names like Beech Great, Black Pins, Buttery Hatch, California, Drysiog, Gelly-dywyll, Pen-tips, Primrose, Soap, Sychffos and many more.

Mining was, and still is, a dangerous occupation and fatalities could occur in the levels as well as in the deep mines:

1853 January 8th Trynant Level, person killed R.D. Hablett haulier boy.

1853 March 2nd Place Level Blackwood, person killed Thomas Morgan labourer.

1853 June 9th Penycoedcae Level Crumlin, person killed Evan Rees collier.

1860 April 22nd Penyfan Mine owners T. Powell and son, person killed Evan Williams collier age 19 fall of roof.

1861 Mine Level Pontypool William Jones miner age 42, fall of stone.

1861 July 17th Trynant Level owner Martin Morison, John Miles age 40, killed by fall of roof in ripping back the old level.

1865 December 28th Gwrhay, owner Roger Lewis, Phillip Williams collier age 45 killed by fall of rubbish.

1869 April 21st New Cwmdows Level, person killed Thomas D. Morgan, collier age 35.

1891 June 4th Penyfan Mine person killed Henry Gilbert, hitcher age 19, contrary to special rules and orders he was riding down a self acting incline on the side of a steep hill on the surface, on approaching halfway the trams climbed the rails and toppled over, his head was crushed under one of the trams.

1906 December 7th Ty-mawr Level, person killed John Thomas age 40.

There were many, many more miners I could add to this list.

The reports of Inspectors of Mines in 1891 show what actions were taken for disobeying the rules of the mine:

At Blackwood Police Court, one miner was fined 1 Guinea, including costs, on 6 February for sleeping in the mine while in charge of safety lamps, with another fined 2 Guineas including costs on 26 June for the same offence. Another miner was fined 2 Guineas and 8 Shillings costs for being in the mine under the influence of drink.

In the following cases apologies were printed and posted up at the colliery with payment into the poor box by the men themselves; for ill treating a horse 20s, for failing to sprag his working face 1s, for neglecting his working place 2s6d, for not reporting a fall which impeded ventilation 2s6d, for exposing a horse to injury 20s, for neglecting their horses three hauliers each find 10s and two hauliers each 5s.

Near Risca on the eastern side of the Ebbw Valley lies the Darran Level Mine, which was in existence in 1843, although no level of that name was listed in 1854. It appears again in 1869 when a Darran mine is listed and owned by Jane Jones. In 1896 the mine employed twenty-one workers underground and three on the surface mining fireclay and coal. By 1908 Darran Firebrick Works Co. Risca owned the mine, with only seven workers underground and four on the surface. In 1921 the mine was still owned by the same company but it closed the following year. It was then reopened by W.O. Padfield to work fireclay, finally closing in 1942. The photograph is one of the headings next to the old Monmouthshire canal.

Another of the Darran Level entrances; a gate has been put on by the Coal Authority for safety reasons.

We are looking inside the fully brick-lined mine. In this photo and the previous one you can see the workmanship that went into the job.

This the third and final of the Darran entrances with another gate on it.

When you look at this photograph, apart from the water, you will notice that this entrance was stone-lined as opposed to brick-lined. I don't know if there was any reason for this.

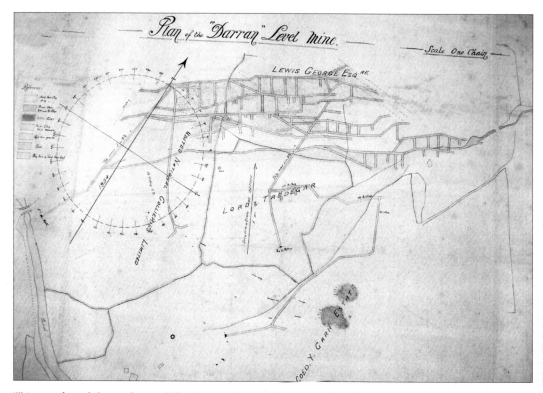

This is a plan of the workings of the Darran Mine. At the left middle of the plan you can see the first entrance featured right by the Monmouthshire canal.

We have now moved a few miles up the valley to the Newbridge area. In this old photograph a coal merchant is loading his coal from a wagon in a siding with the name of the Twyn-Gwyn Colliery on it. The level had been around for many, many years and in 1896 the level was owned by the Twyn-Gwyn Colliery Co. Ltd (Richards) Newbridge, with a workforce of eleven men underground and one on the surface working the Mynyddislwyn seam of coal. The thickness of the upper coal was 3ft 6ins, the lower coal was 2ft 4ins. In 1908, the workforce had increased to twenty-seven men underground and ten on the surface, with John Hope as the manager. Twyn-Gwyn Colliery No. 1 Level was abandoned in 1916, but the name carried on with No. 2 and in 1925 the workforce had increased to 110, quite a sizable number. There is little remaining of this level and if you did not know where to look you would miss the little that does.

Rhiw Level, Crumlin

Rhiw Level, Cwm Kendon, on the west side of the valley which links Crumlin with Croespenmaen. The level was owned in 1923 by the Rhiw Colliery Co.Ltd, per Edwards Bros, and employed thirteen miners. In 1938 it employed six men underground and one on the surface working the Mynyddislwyn seam. It closed in 1974, with Everett Goff being the last owner. In this old photograph the miners, with their horse, have just come out of the mine. It looks like one of them is smoking a cigarette and one a pipe; on their hats the lamps are called a peg and ball lamp. Regulations were a lot more relaxed in those days.

We are now overlooking Aberbeeg and this is the Cwmnant-y-gwynt Level. A level of this name is shown on the John Prugean map of 1843, showing the iron works and collieries. On that particular map a tunnel is shown from Cwmnant-y-gwynt to Trinant Colliery so that the coal could be transported through Trinant and then connect to the tramway which had been constructed by Sir Thomas Protheroe to connect the collieries with the canal company tramroad at Crumlin. The 1880 map shows a tramway had been constructed from Cwmnant-y-gwynt along the side of the mountain, then down to Glan-y-dwr just above Llanhilleth. In 1876 it was listed as owned by James Patrick, and was taken over by the Penyfan Coal Co. in 1880, and in 1888 was owned by T. Williams. In 1896 only two men were employed working the Mynyddislwyn seam. The photo shows the entrance to the mine. Now nothing of this exists anymore – another piece of history has gone.

Two photographs inside the level which I managed to take before it all disappeared forever – a wonderful bit of stonework.

We have moved up the Ebbw Fach Valley towards Cwm near Ebbw Vale. This is the Graig Fawr Red Ash Level. The headings were driven into the mountainside to work the Red Ash seam of coal. In 1918 it employed 126 men underground and eleven on the surface. In 1923 there was a workforce of seventy-five men. On 2 July 1891, George Holwey lost his life in a fall of the roof near the face of a wide stall – it crashed out two of the four props which were set there. This photo shows the mouth of the level and directly above it, just visible through the trees, the airshaft to the level.

Inside the level, the wall is keeping some of the water inside. The level closed in 1928.

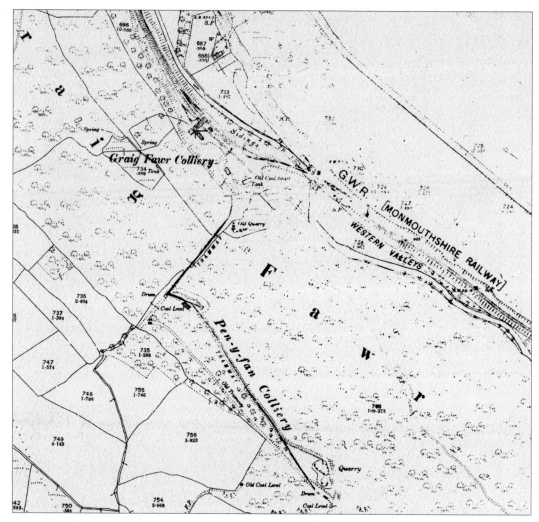

Up above the Graig Fawr Red Ash Level was the Pen-y-fan Colliery working the Mynyddislwyn seam of coal. There were a number of levels with this name dating as far back as 1808, and in 1896 it was owned by Christopher Pond Blackwood, employing twenty-three men underground and five on the surface. This map shows the levels with the tramway that was built to transport the coal down the side of the mountain to the valley floor. The Graig Fawr Colliery shown on this map was a shaft, and the Red Ash Level was a little further up the valley.

Opposite above: On the previous page the map shows there was a tramway, and by the tramway was a drum. This photo shows the drum or wheel that was part of the apparatus that the rope which the drams were connected to travelled around. You can also see part of a stone wall that housed the engine.

Opposite below: The tramway came down from the top level, along the flat part between the trees then went down the side of the mountain to the valley floor. It was a self-acting incline which meant the full drams going down would pull the empty drams back up again, with a passing place for the drams about halfway or a double set of rails all the way.

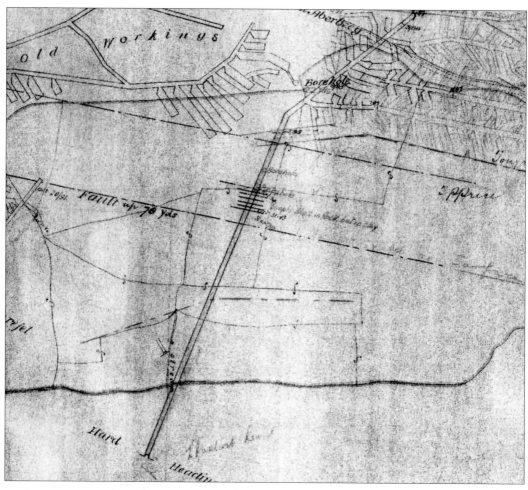

This is a portion of the underground plan of the Peny-y-fan Colliery. At the foot of the plan you can see the words 'Hard Heading' – this was driven into the side of the mountain, over 200 yards in length. This heading was being driven in 1893 and probably a lot earlier; if you look at the plan in September 1893, they were about halfway to the fault which was reached in November 1897. Also on the plan you will see 'From Aberbeeg'; for the local reader this was the lane that branched off the road that came up from Aberbeeg, just before you get to Penyfan pond, and then carries on to Manmoel.

Opposite above and below: On the plan in the previous image the label 'Hard Heading' was seen. We are inside the mine and these two photographs, taken before the mine was sealed, show the actual Hard Heading. It was driven through solid rock and the men who did this must have worked extremely hard, with only hand boring drills to bore the holes for blasting. When I took these photos, you could still see some of the boreholes that were left.

We are now in the Sirhowy Valley, just above Blackwood, and this is Cwrt-y-bella Level. It started its life around the year 1838 with Sir Thomas Phillips and Co., and worked the Mynyddyslwyn coal seam. It opened and closed a number of times, finally being worked as a small licensed mine from the NCB in the 1970s when it was owned by W.J. and A.J. Williams. The following is an extract sent to me by Tony Cooke:

1. Cwrt-y-bella 1840s (working in 1842 Sir Thomas Phillips, 130 employed,–c.e.c1842) 2. Cwrt-y-bella 1964–75 (license from 1.6.1964, terminated 31.3.1975) 13.12.1974 abandoned (Although still listed for 1975). 1969 small mines survey of opencast potential, Cwrt-y-bella, seam heavily worked 60 feet of drift remote area and three sets of electric mains over the coal near the crop, opencasting would not be economic.

This photograph shows the entrance to the level.

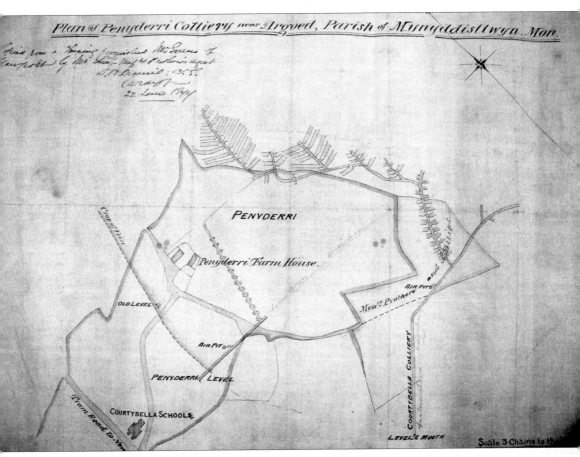

Plan of Penderri Colliery near Argoed, around 1844. This colliery was next to Cwrt-y-bella, and on another plan the two levels were connected underground.

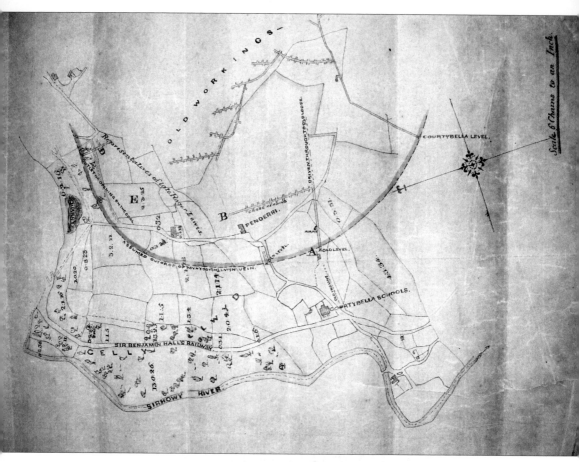

We now have a very early map of the area around Cwrt-y-bella and Penderri, and on it you can see the levels, the outcrop of the coal seam and Sir Benjamin Hall's Tramway (labelled 'Railway') to which these two levels used to be connected. The tramway had been built as far as the Waterloo Colliery by the end of 1811 but the remainder to Hafod-yr-ysclawdd Level was not finished until around 1814. Some of the levels connected to the tramway included Manmoel, Gwrhay, Penycoedcae, Llys-Pentwyn, Tycelyn and Church Farm, plus a few more.

Opposite above and below: Inside Cwrt-y-bella Level, the stone-work still in fine shape.

94

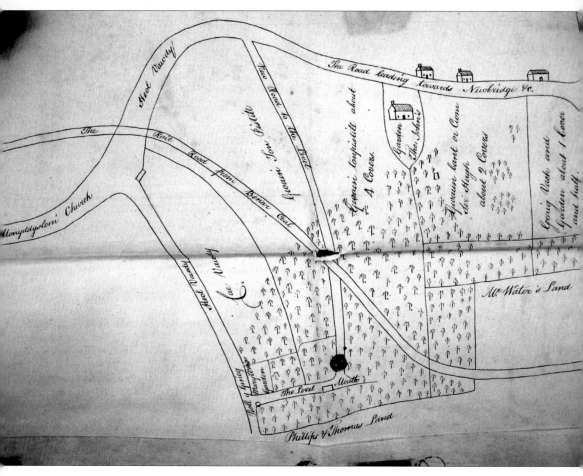

This is the start of two levels; the following extract shows the agreement between the land owner and the owner who wants to open a mine on his land:

> The first is an agreement dated the 2 February 1799 between Samuel Glover of Abercarne in the County of Monmouth Esquire Lord of the Manor of Abercarne and Evan Phillips of Castleton and William Thomas of Coedkernew in the same county for the purpose of opening a colliery sinking a pit and driving of a level in a certain place called Cwm Sir Hugh and under certain pieces of meadow or pastures of land called Gwain y Pistille, Coed Gwain y Pistille, Graig Vach, Gwain Cant and Ca Vardy being in the parish of Mynyddislwyn for a period of 31 years.

I have included the map of where the level was but I leave it up to the reader to work out the exact place – remember this was in the year of 1799 and a lot has changed since then.

The second level is in the Sirhowy Valley, called the Gwrhay or Gwrhai. On this page we have a document dated 19 November 1841 – it is a lease from Mr Richard Perkins the younger to Mr Roger Lewis to extract coal under part of a farm called Gwrhai Vawr.

Below: This document is from Mr John Reid, again to Roger Lewis, to extract coal from under part of a farm called Gwrhai Vawr and under part of a farm called Penyfan Uchaf, both in the county of Monmouth. The level that Mr Roger Lewis wanted to open started behind Oakdale Colliery by the Darran Felin Farm and the workings went up beyond Penyfan pond.

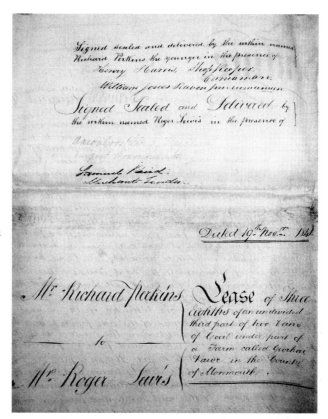

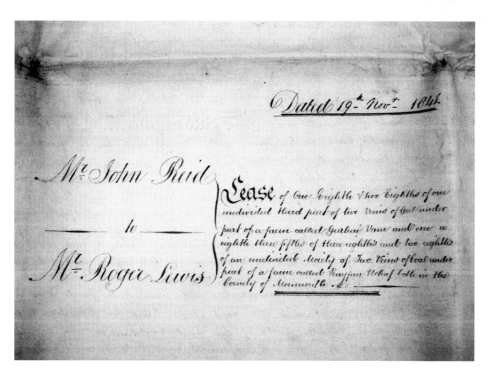

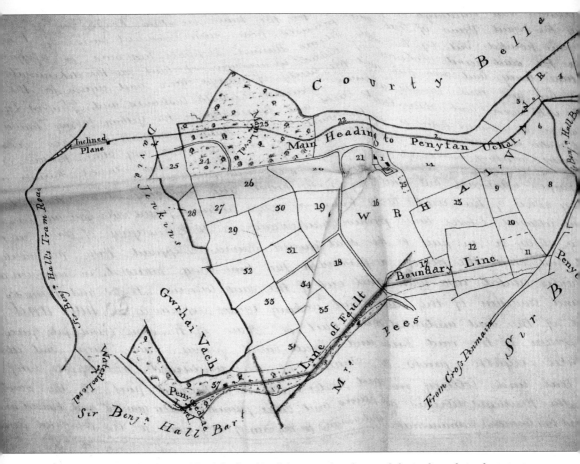

A map which shows the mouth of the level and the main heading and the incline plane that went down to Sir Benjamin Hall's Tramway. Also shown is the position of Waterloo and Penycoedcae Levels.

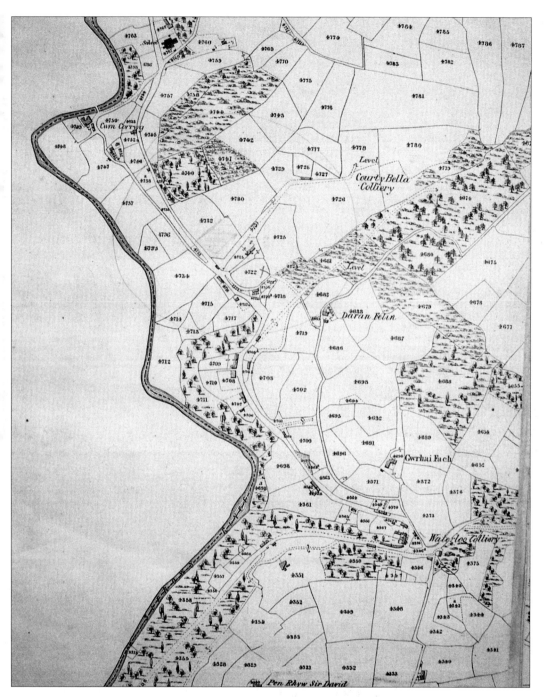

A map from around 1843. If you look at the map where the Court-y-Bella Colliery is shown and the Darran Felin Farm, in-between you can see the Gwrhai Level that has been previously mentioned.

We now come to New Hollybush Colliery Level, which was unique in that the coal saw the light of day before it went up a shaft. Although the Old Hollybush Colliery had a shaft, the coal from the New Hollybush came from a level on the other side of the valley across the river. Headings were driven into the mountainside and the coal came out of the level then across the river via a tramway and into an opening which connected to the shaft of the Old Hollybush Colliery. The coal was then raised up to the level of the old L.& N.W.R. line (Sirhowy branch) and the surface of the colliery so the coal could be screened and loaded. In 1896 it was owned by the executors of the estate of the late E.D. Williams Blackwood, and in 1908 was still under the same ownership. It employed (between the old and the new mines) 146 men underground and twelve on the surface. The collieries closed in 1921, but in July 1929 the Tredegar Co. anticipated water trouble in their mines, and reopened the Hollybush to a distance of 700 yards and installed low lift centrifugal pumps. The idea was to protect the Llanover, Abernant, and Waterloo pits. In 1947 Hollybush was still pumping for Markham Colliery.

Opposite above: We are now further up the Sirhowy Valley and this is Manmoel Colliery, the colliery opened around the year 1813 by Sir Benjamin Hall son-in-law of Richard Crawshay of Cyfartha. In 1869 it was owned by Thomas Phillips Price, while in 1896 C. Pond was the owner with a workforce of seventeen underground and five on the surface. In 1947 there was a small mine working under licence from the NCB called Manmoel, owned by W. and T. Bowditch.

Opposite below: Inside the mine, with the usual body of water that plagued a lot of the mines.

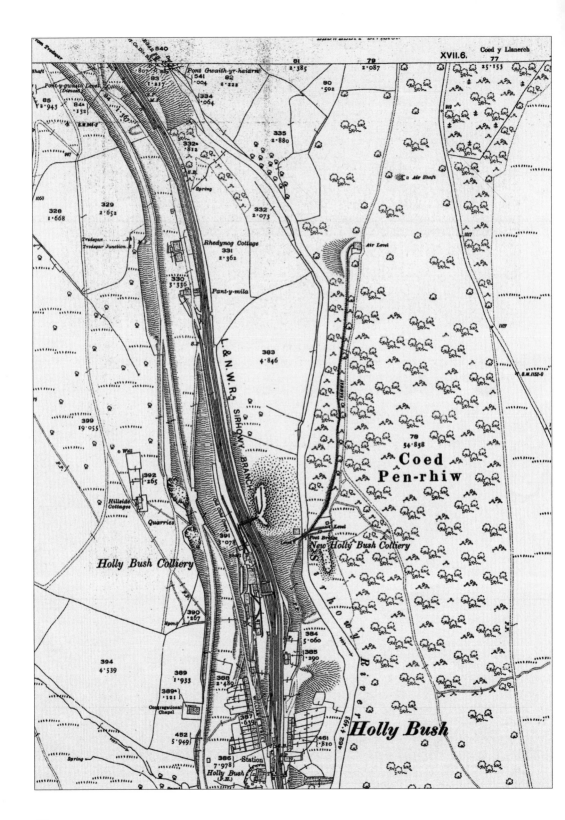

A very old photograph of the miners, horses and drams of the New Hollybush just coming down the tramway from the level before crossing over the river to the shaft of the Old Hollybush.

Opposite: This is a map from around 1920 and on it you can clearly see the Old and the New Hollybush, as well as the tramway.

Two photographs which show the main intake road, half-filled with water, and the return airway which are both shown on the map from around 1920.

The coal seam of the level with a long-abandoned shovel.

There were a number of exits to the level as it worked the seam of coal going up the valley, and this was the last but one near the village of Troedrhiwgwair.

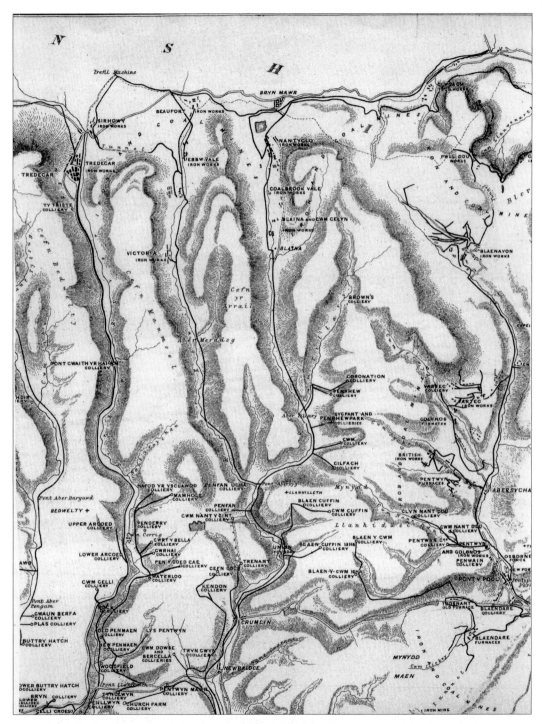

John Prujean's map of the iron works and collieries and their means of communications by railway, tram road and canal, published in 1843. You can see quite a few of the collieries and levels mentioned.

We now move to the Glyn Valley which runs between Hafodyrynys and Pontypool. In this valley were numerous openings from shafts to levels and after months of searching, this level was shown to me by Stuart Poultney. It is the Glyn Level No. 2, owned in 1880 by the Blaendare Co., and the photograph shows the inside of the level. There was also Glyn Level No. 1 a little further on to the west of the valley.

This is a photograph of the inside of a level very close to the Glyn and shows the type of stone-work that was used.

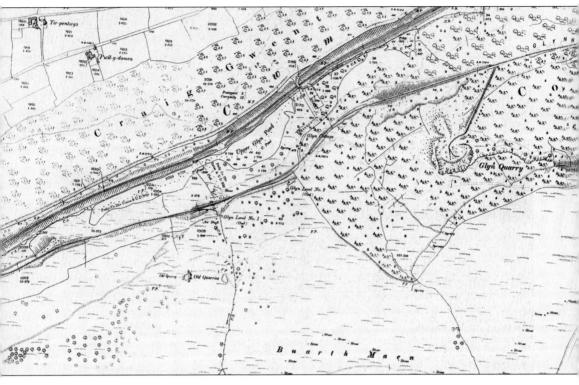

A map from around 1901 showing the Glyn Valley, including Glyn Level No. 1 and No. 2. You can also see Glyn Quarry on the map – this was near where the Quarry Level would eventually open.

Opposite above: The Quarry Level, which was a little further on towards Pontypool, was opened around 1912 by the Blaendare Co Ltd. In 1918 it employed 103 men, including twenty on the surface. It was the scene of rioting during a lockout in the 1926 general strike and several men were arrested, including Arthur Jenkins, the miners' agent and father of the late Lord Jenkins of Hillhead. It closed in the early 1940s; a gate is over the entrance for safety.

Opposite below: The inside of the level, lined with brick as opposed to stone in the previous level.

The Mountain Level Blaendare upper race, this level worked the Elled coal seam. Richard Dobbs lost his life in this mine in 1846 – his wife was worried that he hadn't come home and when they checked they found the roof had collapsed. When the fall was cleared they found him dead. It was a sad fact that the woman had also lost her first husband, Lewis Howell, in 1836 by a roof fall at the same mine. In 1883 W. Gadd, aged seventeen, also lost his life at this mine.

Inside the level again, brick-lined and in wonderful condition considering its age. Some of the old rails were left in place.

Above and below: We are now in the Afan Lwyd Valley between Pontypool and Blaenafon around the Llanerch Colliery area and I came upon these two openings by chance. There is no mention of the names of these levels on the old Ordnance Survey maps but there was the old Greenland Mine working this area in 1862, not to be confused with the later Greenland Colliery.

Deakins Slope Talywaun opened in 1899. In 1925, J. Viponds & Co. Ltd took to running it and in 1938 they employed 372 men; in 1947 this had risen to 549, but by 1955 the manpower was 317 with the output at 79,000 tons. It worked the Garw Big Yard, Meadow, and Elled seams of coal, but it was closed by the NCB in 1957. The photo shows the entrance with the central locking stone having a date on it of 1899. The old drams are typical of the type used in the mine.

Opposite above and below: We are still in the Llanerch Colliery area and although I cannot name this particular level, the ones that were working around here many years ago included Morrison's, Greenland Colliery, Graig-Ddu, Baileys Slope, Crop Level and clay levels, as well as the deep mines such as Blaenserchan, Gwenallt, Cwm-nant-ddu, Glyn-nant-ddu and, of course, the Llanerch Colliery, where in 1890 an explosion occurred killing 176 men and boys.

This is the remains of an engine which served the coal and quarry industries. These particular remains are above the Garden Festival shopping site near Ebbw Vale and we are looking down the valley with the old tramway clearly showing towards Cwm. On the 1901 Ordnance Survey map it shows the engine and a tramway leading from the quarry and levels down to the Victoria blast furnaces.

Opposite above and below: I found this mine by accident while out walking – it's at the top of the valley by Brynmawr and has the appearance of a mine that the miners just walked away from. The dram and the rails are still there and an engine still in the shed; just a memory of what was.

We have now switched valleys again and have gone back to the Sirhowy Valley up by the village of Bedwellty Pits. High up on the western side of the valley are these remains of the engine and drum used to transport the stone from Bedwellty quarries and coal from the Bedwellty Levels down the side of the mountain to Bedwellty Pit, which was next to the village. The levels were working in 1896 with a workforce of twenty-eight and was under the ownership of the Tredegar Iron and Coal Co. Ltd.

3

THE REMAINING
WORKING LEVELS

We now come to the only working levels left in Gwent. Will there be any more or is this the end of an era? Where there use to be hundreds we are down to the last two. Is there plenty of coal left underground? If you talk to the old miners they would say yes, there is lots of coal left down there. I can not envisage them opening any deep mines, and it will never be 'King Coal' again, but hopefully there will be a market for the levels to operate in. However, to open a new level would be very expensive with all the health and safety laws about today, plus the environmental issues which seems to be the main topic. Something may have to give, because we cannot rely on oil or gas forever.

Blaentillery Mine No. 2 on the hillside above Big Pit Blaenafon working the top coal. The seam is between 2-3ft thick and has a face 50m in length, with a cutter undercutting the coal. When I visited the mine it had a workforce of six men and had been owned for the last two years by Thomas Martin Mining Ltd. This photograph shows the surface of the mine and a lorry being loaded. The mine was featured in the television programme *Coal House*.

A cold winter's scene showing the mine and the countryside looking north that surrounds it. In the distance you can see the track that led from the mine to the main road and came out by Llanelly Hill between Blaenafon and Brynmawr.

The coal has travelled out of the mine by conveyor belt and is tipped on the ground ready to be loaded.

A nice, warm coal fire to dry your wet clothes after coming out of the mine.

Opposite below: Three of the Blaentillery miners have just finished their shift and are just outside the entrance to the mine; notice their wet gear and knee pads.

Two of the Blaentillery miners Adrian Durham and Alan Stevens, having finished their shift drying their wet clothes in front of the fire. The other miners, Malcolm Lias, Gwyn Woodland, Dai Callaghan, Huw Thomas and the mine manager are still in the mine.

Black Barn Level, the second of the only remaining working levels left in Gwent, is situated behind and to the north of the village of Pantygaseg. It has been owned since 2001 by Gareth Thomas. A scene showing the surface of the mine; you can see the rail tracks coming out of the supply heading.

Opposite above: The conveyor that transported the coal out from the mine a lot quicker than the drams did; this was the intake side of the mine.

Opposite below: The Blaentillery Mine was a lot different on the surface than other mines, in that quite a lot of it had a large covered area and this photo shows the drams under that cover going towards the return airway roadway.

A conveyor was installed at this mine to bring the coal to the surface, as you can see here with a small quantity of coal outside the mine.

Looking towards the return roadway entrance with the rails disappearing into the level.

A tippler or tumbler is shown here on a cold winter's morning waiting for the miners to come back to work. A flat bogey with a bar-hook is holding it, which was a metal safety bar that was attached to the dram which trailed along the ground behind the dram to stop it moving backwards.

Looking into the return roadway metal arches in use. On the right-hand side you can see the electric pull box with the wire attached that was used to signal to the driver of the engine which way to pull the drams.

As I was putting the finishing touches to the book I visited the old Johnson Mine, Forgeside, near Blaenafon, which is a level about half a mile down the valley from the Blaentillery Mine and found that there was activity at this mine. Talking to the two miners, Shane Hawkins and Raymond Davis, who have been employed to prepare this mine for reopening, I found that one of them had originally worked there before when it was last worked in the 1990s, The original mine had been abandoned in 1998 and was listed Abandoned (reported on care and maintenance, not reached production by 12.10.1997, no work since 23.5.1998 and abandoned 28.5.1998. Owner B.J. Llewellyn). We now find that the Johnson Mine is going to reopen under the ownership of Riche Uk Mining Ltd; they hope to open the mine late spring or early summer and will work the Big Vein, then if all goes well later on drive through the fault to reach a seam of coal 4-6ft in height so by the time this book is published there could be three working mines in Gwent. This is a sign at the entrance to the mine.

The two entrances to the Johnson Mine.

The twenty-first century approach to level working at the Johnson Mine – if the old miners could see this!

Other titles published by The History Press

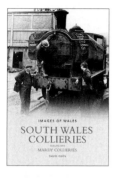

South Wales Collieries – Volume Five: Mardy
DAVID OWEN

This is part of a series on South Wales Collieries, which illustrates the area's industrial history during the past 200 years, in text and photographs, and gives a glimpse of both working and village life in the valleys. David Owen provides over 200 images of miners, theur housing and the colleries that once provided employment for tens of thousands and that have now all but dissapeared.

978 0 7524 3251 9

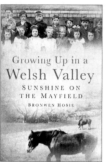

Growing up in a Welsh Valley: Sunshine on the Mayfield
BRONWEN HOSIE

This compendium of nostalgic tales about Dai Morrissey, the author's father, as he grows up in the Rhymney Valley will bring both tears of joy and sadness to the reader. It starts at the end of the First World War when Dai was four years old, and continues through his childhood years, to when he was a young adult leaving the mines and starting his own business. This book captures wonderful memories of family life, hilarious adventures with friends, and the sadness Dai felt on losing others in the pit.

978 0 7524 4756 8

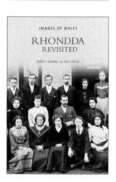

Rhondda Revisited
EMRYS JENKINS AND ROY GREEN

This absorbing collection of old images offers a nostalgic glimpse into the history of the Rhondda Valley during the last century. Many aspects of everyday life are featured, from schools and churches, public houses and shops – the double-decker buses taking the workers to Alfred Polikoff's and local sporting derbies between Treherbert and Treorchy are also featured – to the carnival bands, the Saturday matinees and the local residents who have proudly called the Rhondda their home.

978 0 7524 3388 2

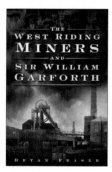

The West Riding Miners and Sir William Garforth
BRYAN FRASER

Today, many thousands of miners owe their lives to the work of Sir William E. Garforth and his staff of the West Riding Colliery. Written in a distinctive narrative style, this book provides a wonderfully detailed account of how Garforth revolutionised the mining industry's safety and rescue procedures. It also reveals the sacrifices that were made by the local community, especially the miners, who dedicated their lives in order to improve those of future generations.

978 0 7524 4991 3

Visit our website and discover thousands of other History Press books.

www.thehistorypress.co.uk